AF507174

Printed by Kiyanni B., Write It Out Publishing, LLC. in the United States of America.

ISBN: 979-8-3492-0947-5
LCCN: 2024926965
Book Cover Illustrator: Rumana Rupa
Editor: Renee Johnson

First printing, (paperback) © December 2024
by Mary Lucas Blunt
Virginia Beach, Virginia
Werfamily41@verizon.net

Talking to God: What is God Saying to You

VIRGINIA BEACH, VA

Talking to God:
What is God Saying to You

Mary Lucas Blunt

From the time we are young, we are taught that God is always watching over us. We are told that we can pray to God for guidance and protection, and that God will listen to us. But as we grow older, we may start to feel disconnected from God or unsure of how to communicate with Him.

This book is designed to help children develop a deeper connection with God through prayer and conversation. Each chapter contains a conversation between a child and God, addressing a different topic or question. Through these conversations, children can learn how to talk to God, and how to listen for His guidance and wisdom.

- Mary Lucas Blunt

God's Love

Noah : God, do you really love me?

GOD : Yes, my child, I love you very much.
         I love you more than you can imagine.

Noah : How do you love me?

GOD : I love you unconditionally, just as you are. I love you when you're happy and when you re sad. I love you when you make mistakes, and when you do your best.

Noah : Can I feel your love?

GOD : Yes, you can. My love is all around you in the people you care about, in the beauty of nature, and in the kindness of strangers. If you look for it, you will always find it.

Bible Verse: John 15:17
This is My command. Love each other.

Noah : God, I need your help. I'm having a hard time at school.

GOD : I'm here for you, my child. What do you need help with?

6

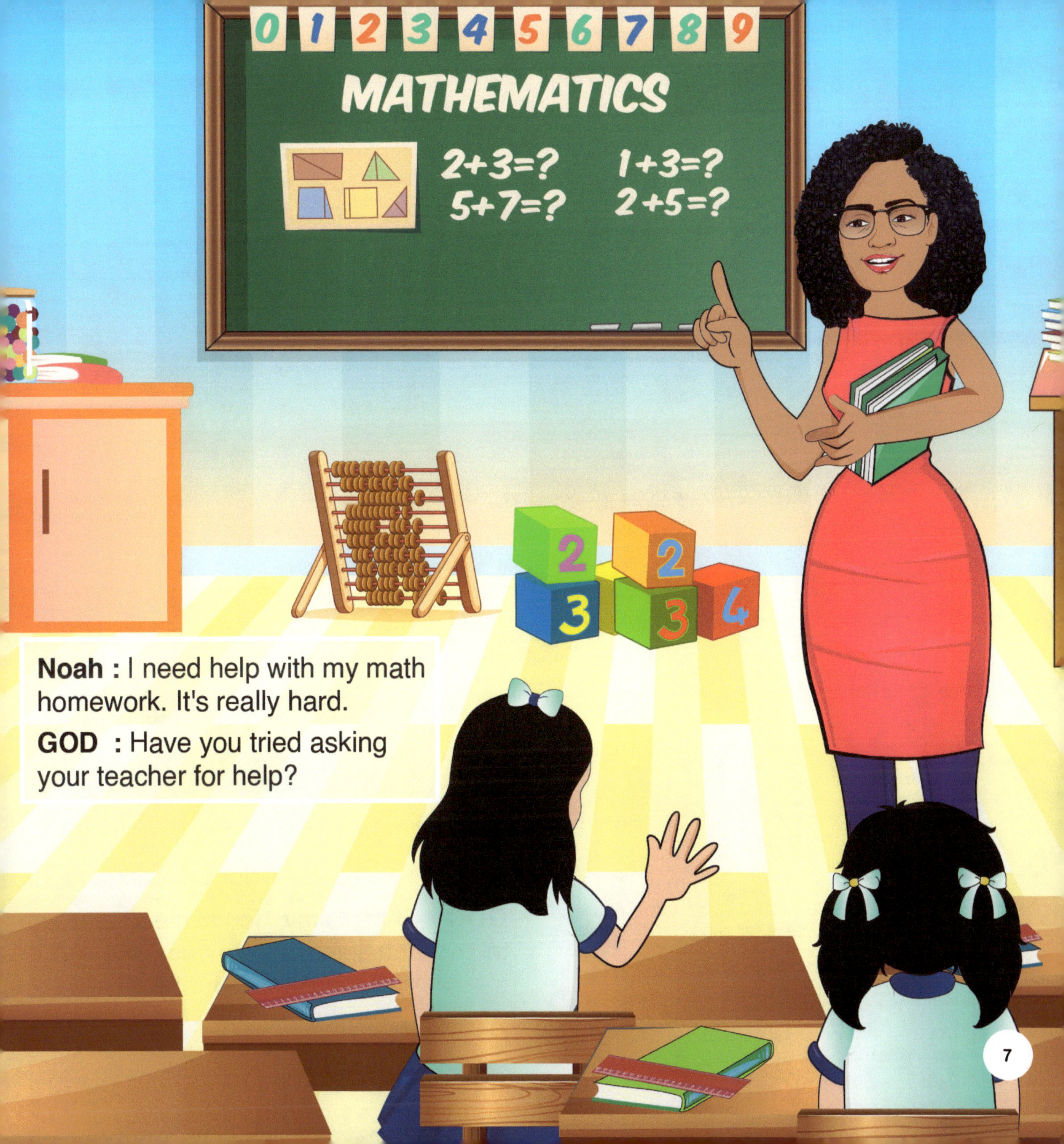

Noah : I need help with my math homework. It's really hard.

GOD : Have you tried asking your teacher for help?

Noah : Yes, but I still don't understand.

GOD : That's okay. Sometimes, we need to ask for help more than once. Have you tried asking a classmate for help?

Noah : No, I haven't.

GOD : Maybe you can work together on your homework. And remember, I'm always here for you, too.

Bible Verse: Isaiah 41:13
I am the Lord your God. I am holding your right hand. And I tell you, "Don't be afraid, I will help you."

Forgiveness

Noah : God, I did something bad. Will you forgive me?

GOD : Of course, my child. I forgive you.

Noah : How do I know you've forgiven me?

God : You can feel it in your heart. When you ask for forgiveness, you are showing that you are sorry for what you did. And when you feel forgiven, you can let go of the guilt and move on.

Noah : Does that mean I don't have to be punished?

God   : Sometimes, there are consequences for our actions, but forgiveness means that you are not defined by your mistakes. You can learn from them and make better choices in the future.

Bible Verse: Mathew 6:14
Yes, if you forgive others for the things they do wrong, then your father in heaven will forgive you for the things you do wrong.

Gratitude

Noah : God, what does it mean to be grateful?

God : Being grateful means appreciating the good things in your life. It means noticing the blessings and joys around you, even when things are difficult.

Noah : What are some things I can be grateful for?

God : You can be grateful for your family and friends, for the food you eat and the clothes you wear, for the beauty of nature, and for the opportunities you have to learn and grow.

Noah : How can I show my gratitude?

God : You can say thank you, you can do something kind for someone else, and you can take care of the things you have been given. When you show gratitude, you create more happiness and positivity in the world.

Bible Verse: Isaiah 4:4
Everything that God made is good. Nothing that God made should be refused if it is accepted with thanks to God.

Trust

Noah : God, how can I trust you when bad things happen?

God   : I know it can be hard to trust me when things don't go the way you want them to. But remember that I am always with you, even in the difficult times. I will never abandon you, and I will always guide you towards the right path.

Noah : But why do bad things happen in the first place?

God : There are many reasons why bad things happen, my child. Sometimes, it's because of choices that people make, sometimes, it's because of natural events that are beyond our control, and sometimes, it's because of the consequences of our own actions. But no matter what, I am always here to comfort you and help you find your way through the challenges.

Noah : How can I learn to trust you more?

God : One way to build trust is to spend time with me every day. You can pray, read the Bible or other holy texts, or simply talk to me in your heart. When you feel my presence, you will know that you can always count on me.

Bible Verse: Isaiah 26:4
So, trust the Lord always. Trust the Lord for he is our rock forever.

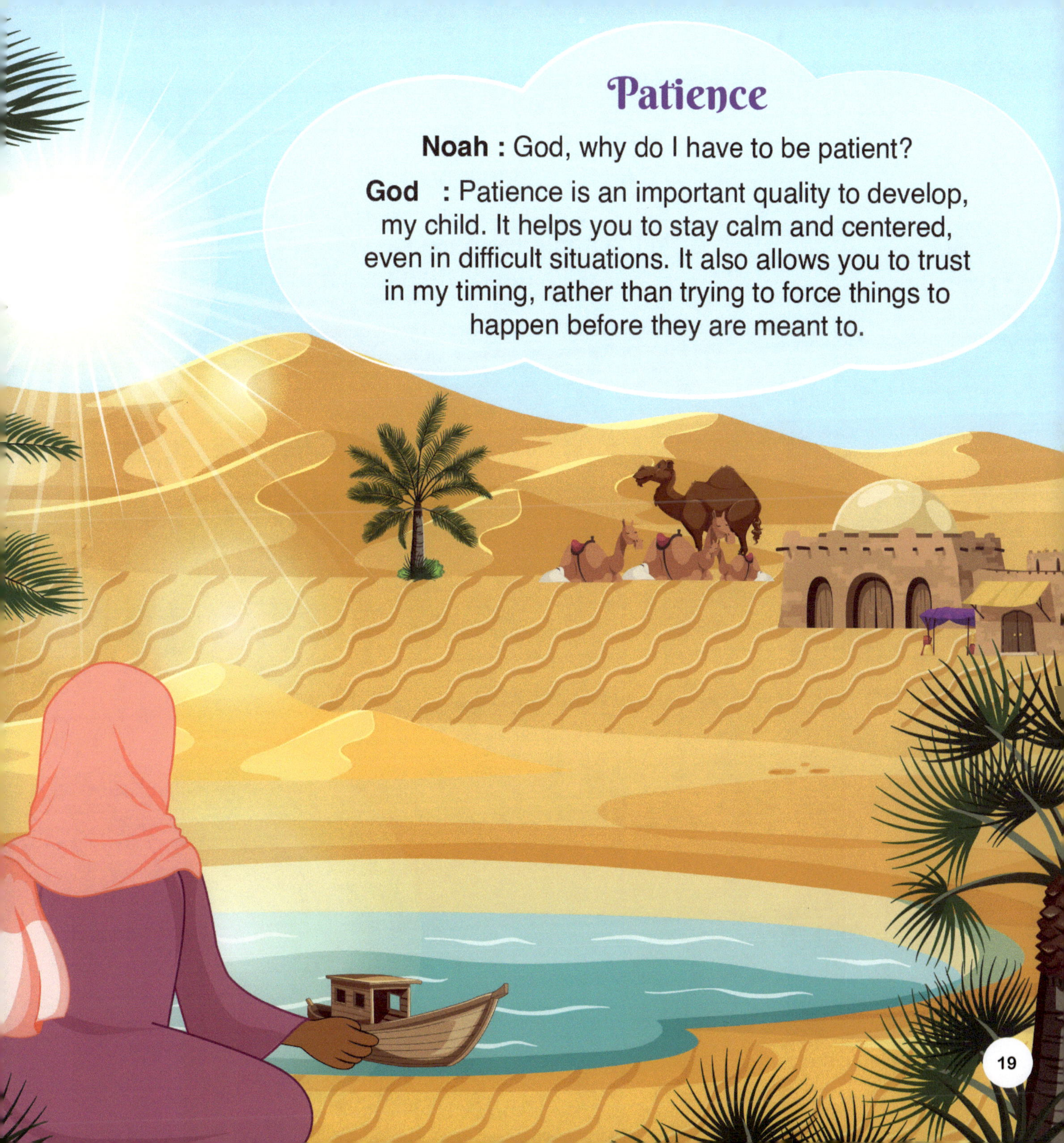

Patience

Noah : God, why do I have to be patient?

God : Patience is an important quality to develop, my child. It helps you to stay calm and centered, even in difficult situations. It also allows you to trust in my timing, rather than trying to force things to happen before they are meant to.

19

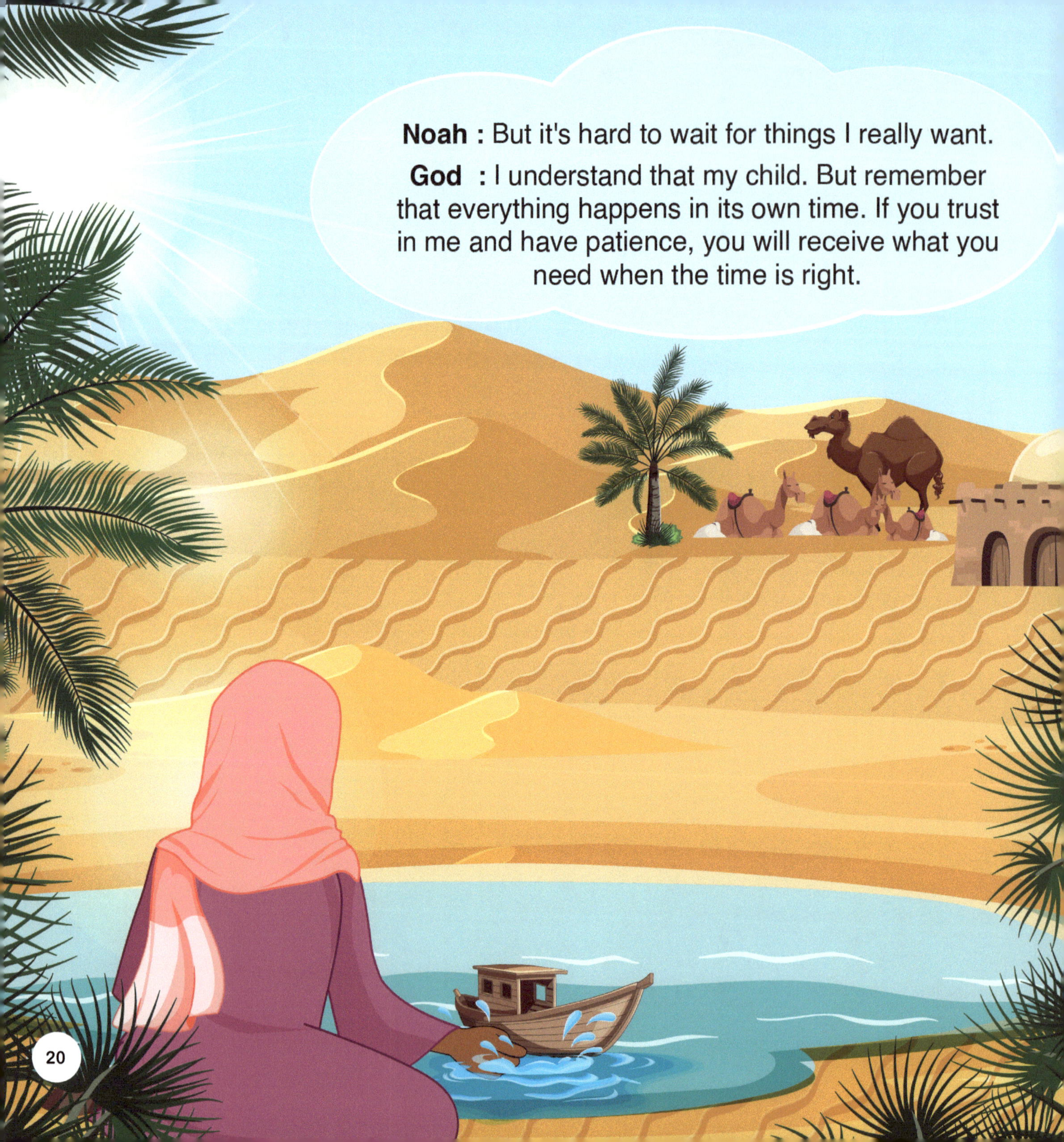

Noah : But it's hard to wait for things I really want.
God : I understand that my child. But remember that everything happens in its own time. If you trust in me and have patience, you will receive what you need when the time is right.

Noah : How can I practice patience?

God : You can practice patience by taking deep breaths when you feel frustrated, by reminding yourself that everything happens for a reason, and by focusing on the present moment instead of worrying about the future. You can also pray for patience and ask me to help you cultivate this important virtue.

Bible Verse: James 1:4
Let your patience show perfectly in what you do. Then you will be perfect and complete. You will have everything you need.

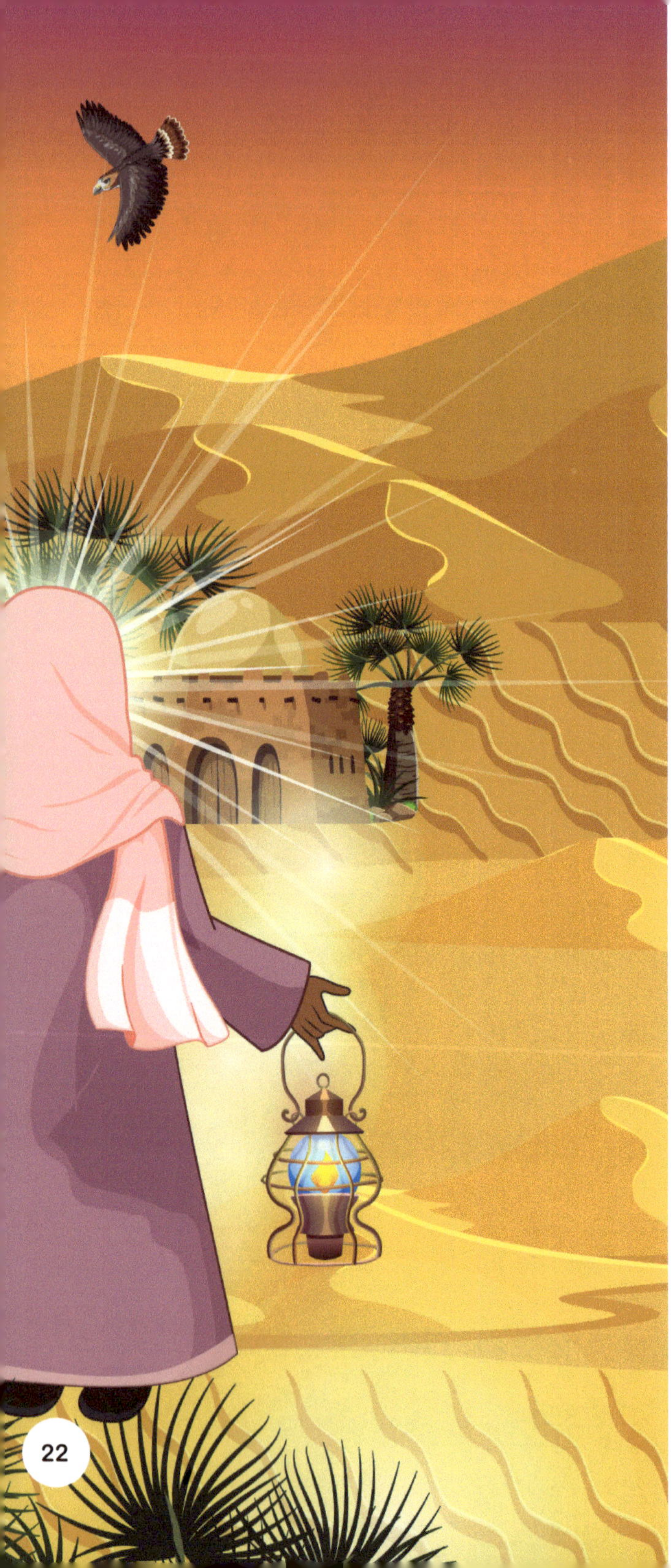

Noah : God, how can I be brave when I'm scared?

God : Courage comes from trusting in me, my child. When you know that I am with you, you can face any challenge with strength and confidence.

Noah : But what if I still feel afraid?

God : It's okay to feel afraid, my child. But remember that fear is just a feeling, and it doesn't have to control you. When you feel afraid, you can pray to me for courage and strength, and you can remember that I am always with you.

Noah : How can I develop more courage?

God : You can develop courage by facing your fears, even in small ways. You can also surround yourself with people who encourage and support you, and who help you to see your own strengths and abilities. And most importantly, you can trust in me and know that I will never let you face anything alone.

Bible Verse: Psalm 56:3
When I am afraid I will trust you.

The Power of Faith

Noah : God, what is faith?

God : Faith is trusting in something you can't see or touch, my child. It's knowing in your heart that I am always with you, even when you can't see me or feel my presence.

Noah : How can I have more faith?

God   : You can have more faith by spending time with me, reading the Bible or other holy texts, and by praying for guidance and strength. When you practice faith, you will feel more connected to me and more confident in your own abilities.

Bible Verse: Hebrews 11:1
Faith means being sure of the things we hope for. And faith means knowing something is real even if we do not see it.

Hope

Noah : God, what is hope?

God : Hope is believing that good things are possible, even in difficult times. It's having faith that things will get better, even when they seem bleak.

Noah : How can I have more hope?

God : You can have more hope by focusing on the positive things in your life, by finding reasons to be grateful, and by trusting in me to guide you towards a brighter future. When you have hope, you have the power to overcome any obstacle.

Bible Verse: Lamentations 3:25
The Lord is good to those who put their hope in him. He is good to those who look to him for help.

Noah : God, why is forgiveness important?

God : Forgiveness is important because it allows you
to let go of negative emotions and move forward in your
life. When you forgive someone, you are showing
compassion and understanding, and you are freeing
yourself from the burden of anger and resentment.

Noah : But what if someone has hurt me really badly?

God : Forgiving someone who has hurt you deeply can be a difficult process, but it is also a powerful way to heal and move forward. When you forgive someone, you are not condoning their actions, but rather releasing them and yourself from the pain of the past.

Bible Verse: Mathew 6:14
Yes if you forgive others for things they do wrong, then your father in heaven will also forgive things you do wrong.

Finding Your Purpose

Noah : God, what is my purpose in life?

God : Your purpose is to live a life that is true to your values and that brings goodness and light into the world. Your purpose may involve helping others, pursuing your passions, or simply being kind and compassionate to those around you.

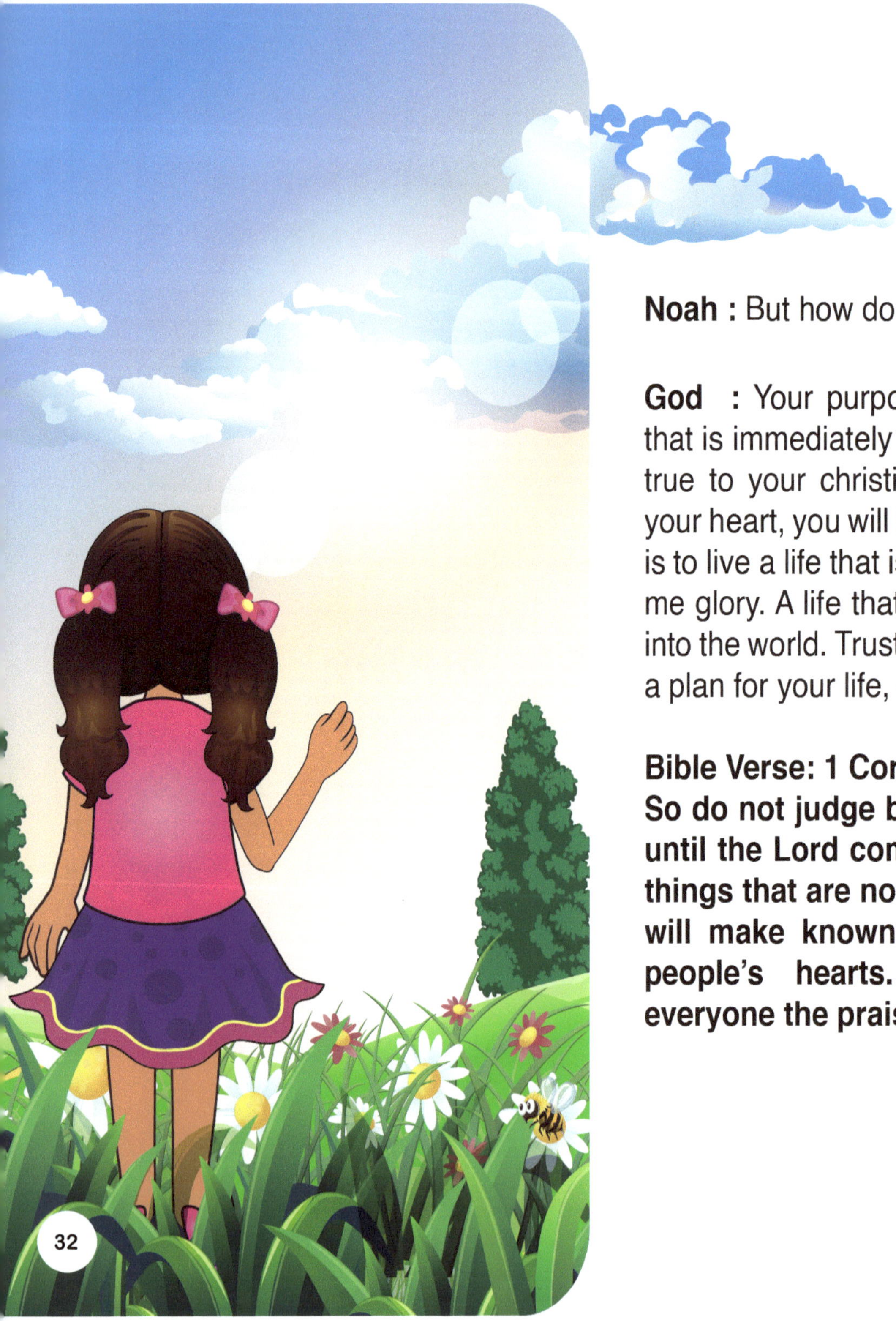

Noah : But how do I know what my purpose is?

God   : Your purpose may not be something that is immediately clear to you, but by staying true to your christian values and listening to your heart, you will find your way. Your purpose is to live a life that is pleasing to me and brings me glory. A life that brings goodness and light into the world. Trust in me and know that I have a plan for your life, even if you can't see it yet.

Bible Verse: 1 Corinthian 4:5
So do not judge before the right time; wait until the Lord comes. He will bring to light things that are now hidden in darkness. He will make known the secret purposes of people's hearts. Then God will give everyone the praise he should get.

Noah : God, what is joy?

God : Joy is the feeling of happiness and contentment that comes from knowing that you are loved and valued. It is the feeling of being connected to something greater than yourself, and of experiencing the beauty and wonder of the world around you.

Noah : How can I experience more joy in my life?

God : You can experience more joy by being present in the moment, by finding ways to serve others and make a positive impact in the world, and by cultivating gratitude and appreciation for the blessings in your life. When you focus on joy, you create more of it in your life and in the lives of those around you.

Bible Verse: Jeremiah 29:11
I say this because I know what I have planned for you, "says the Lord." I have good plans for you. I don't plan to hurt you. I plan to give you hope and a good future.

Talking to God is a powerful way for children to deepen their spiritual connection and find comfort, guidance, and strength in times of need. By developing a regular prayer practice and staying true to their values, children can cultivate a deeper sense of purpose, meaning, and joy in their lives. May this book serve as a helpful resource for children seeking to deepen their relationship with God and find peace, love, and happiness in His embrace.